C# Programming for Beginners

How to Learn C# in Less Than a Week.
The Ultimate Step-by-Step Complete Course
from Novice to Advanced Programmer

William Brown

Table of contents

Introduction

Greetings! fellow programmer who is also discovering the basics. Thank you very much for getting your hands on this book! This book is written to help you learn C# programming swiftly, whether you are an established computer programmer or a total novice. Topics have been carefully chosen to provide you with a detailed introduction to C# while avoiding knowledge overload, but before we get started on this exciting journey, let's answer some basic questions:

Best way to read this book?

When it comes to reading technical books, there is no right or wrong way. It is on the reader how they want to progress. This book has both written and embedded code examples with output which will help understand the working of C# code. Whenever a new programming concept starts, it starts with explaining its syntax and then works its way from there. In this book, the fundamentals of programming are described in detail.

Chapter 1: What is C#?

1.1: What is a programming language?

A programming language, in simple words, is the language of computers. There are numerous computer programming languages out there, and these languages usually have a set of rules the programmer (the person who writes the code) must follow. In other words, a programming language is an artificial language that a computer can understand. There are two significant types of programming languages those are:

- Low-Level Programming languages
- High-Level Programming Languages

Low-level languages are programming languages that contain basic instructions that a computer can understand. Unlike high-level languages utilized by software developers, low-level code is often cryptic, and humans cannot understand it. Assembly language and machine language are two types of low-level programming languages. Software programs and scripts are created in high-level languages, **like C#, C++, Java**. A programmer can create and edit source code in high-level languages using an **IDE** or a text editor. However, a computer can not recognize the code written in a high-level language, so a high-level language is translated into machine code (low-level language).

Assembly language is closer to the computer's understanding when comparing it to high-level languages. It consists of essential English words called commands as ADD (add), SUB (subtract), and MOV (move). These commands carry out fundamental operations, such as reading and writing values to memory registers and performing calculations. Even though assembly language is considered low-level, it still needs to be converted into machine code for computers to understand. For this conversion, we use Assembler.

Next, we have the **Machine language** or **Machine code,** which is known to be the computer's actual language written in computer's architecture. Machine code is usually in binary form, 0 or 1, True or false. Hence, machine code is the lowest level of programming language as the computer understands it without the need of translating or converting. These binary numbers (0s and 1s) combine and form a set of instructions for the computer, so when a programmer writes the code in a high-level language, it is converted to Machine code using an interpreter (interpreter executes the code by code in real-time) or and compiler (compiler first collects all the code, and then performs it).

Now let's talk more about High-level languages, these languages are made for programmers, developers to create programs without understanding the machine code, all high-level language has set of rules the coder needs to follow, each language also has different syntax, some characteristics of high-level languages are:

- High-level languages are close or similar to human speech.

- They are programmer friendly, unlike Low-level language.

- They do not work together directly with the hardware or machine.

In this book, we will be learning to code in C#.

1.2: Introduction to C#

C# (pronounced C-sharp or See-Sharp) is a general-purpose, object-oriented programming language used for a wide range of applications (which we will discuss later in detail). Microsoft announced C # at the "Professional Developers Conference" in July 2000, led by Anders Hejlsberg. This programming language is used to build diverse software and applications using *Microsoft .Net Framework* (Framework is a structure indicating what kind of programs can be made and how they work, some frameworks also include actual programs or offer programming tools) other frameworks like *ASP .Net.* C# code, like all modern programming languages, looks a lot like English, which computers cannot comprehend. Therefore, C# code must be converted into machine language a compiler.

1.3: Why C#?

You might be wondering why C#? That is because C# has a wide range of uses. One can use C# to make video games, scientific apps, web apps, and the list goes on. One advantage of learning C# is its easy-to-understand syntax. C # also has a vast active community working on different projects. If you have any previous programming experience with languages like C++ or Java, you will find learning C# a breeze. And if you are new to the world of programming, C# is one of the best options to learn as a first language as it is constructed to be easy to understand, unlike C or C++.

The following are notable characteristics/features of C#:

1. **Simple language:** C# is a simple language in that it supports a structured approach (by segmenting the problem), a comprehensive set of library functions, and data types, among other features. Additionally, some of the more puzzling C++ concepts are skipped or simplified in C#. For example, C# lacks complex pointers which are found in C++. In C++, the

operators: -->, and references operators are used to denote namespaces, member access, and references, respectively. In C#, on the other hand, a single period or dot (.) operator performs all these functions.

2. **Modern:** C# has developed a reputation as a language for creating **NGWS (*next-generation windows services*)** applications. Memory management is automated in C# and is no longer the programmer's responsibility. C# garbage collector is designed for this automated memory management. Additionally, C# allows cross-language exception management. For monetary calculations, C# introduces a new data form called decimal. Another characteristic of C# is its ability to perform economic calculations. Another contemporary aspect of C# is its robust model support.

3. **Object-Based:** The C# programming language is an object-oriented programming language. OOPs simplifies creation and maintenance, while procedure-oriented programming languages are difficult to handle as projects increase in scale. OOP also enables code reusability and reduces code redundancy. It supports many vital features of object-oriented

programming, including data encapsulation, inheritance, and polymorphism.

4. **Type-safe:** The standard typing system ensures type protection, which increases the reliability of the code. C# implements the following type-safety mechanisms:

- An uninitialized variable cannot be used in C#.

- It ensures that arithmetic operations do not overflow.

- It verifies the array's range and warns when access is out of bounds..

- Objects and arrays that are dynamically allocated are initialized to nil.

- It is compatible with automated garbage collection.

5. **Exception Handling:** The Dot(.) NET framework unifies the way exceptions are handled across languages. Via an integrated and extensible approach, exception management enables the detection and recovery of errors. The C# programming language's exception handling capabilities provide a mechanism for dealing with any unusual or abnormal conditions that might occur while the program is being executed.

There are more features of this programming language, but we will take a look at the basic rules of C# for now.

Basic Rules of C#:

As with any programming language, C# has some syntax rules that must be strictly followed to ensure that the code is appropriately formatted and understandable by the C# compiler:

- **Case sensitivity** – C# is a case-sensitive language, which means that the uppercase letters **"A"** and lowercase **"a"** are two different elements.

- C# does not offer global variables or functions, so everything is wrapped in classes.

- **Termination** – All statements in the C# language must end with a (;) semicolon character, just like all sentences in the English language must end with a (.) Period character.

- **Keywords** – The C# language includes a range of keywords that have a specific syntactic meaning and may not be used to refer to programmer-defined objects in code.

- **Naming conventions** – In C# code, a programmer-defined identifier name can begin with an underscore (_) or a letter in either uppercase or lowercase. Additionally, the term can contain an underscore, alphabets, or digits. Consistent naming conventions are really important as a good programmer. When starting out, one should use simple words to name their variables.

- **Single Line comments** – Brief comments on a single line must begin with / two forward slash characters.

- **Block comments** – Comments that span several lines must begin with the **/*** forward slash and asterisk characters and end with the reverse ***/** asterisk and forward slash characters. Block or multiline comments are really useful for writing a rough outline or algorithm of the code.

Commenting on your code is a considered good practice as frequently you will forget what this part of the code does, and it also helps others when they read your code.

1.4: Choosing an IDE

IDE, an acronym for Integrated Development Environment, is a type of software that includes comprehensive tools that assist programmers as they code. An integrated development environment (IDE) comprises of a text editor, a debugger, and tools for automating the construct process. There are several IDEs to choose from. Most of the time, it is a matter of personal preference. We'll be working with Microsoft's Visual Studio Code (commonly known as VS code), a feature-rich and advanced code editor throughout this book. It is entirely free and open-source, and it supports a wide variety of programming languages. Additionally, it has a marketplace from where one can download different themes and extensions. It also includes code completion suggestions (IntelliSense), which aids in speeding up the coding process by eliminating the need to type the same variables repeatedly.

1.4.1: Configuring Visual Studio Code for use with C#.

In this section, we will set up VS Code for C# by following the steps stated below:

1. The first step is to download the framework. As stated in the introduction, C# uses the .Net framework. Go to the following link to download *.Net Core*. Click on the download button, and the next page will be something like this:

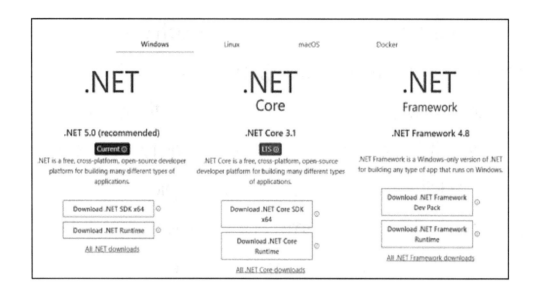

2. Then, on your screen, pick the operating system of your choice. And download the **LTS** (long-term support) or the recommended version. After that, follow the installation instructions you see on the screen. When the installation is complete, press the close button.

3. Next up, we need to install Visual Studio Code from the following link: *Visual Studio Code*:

4. Press the download button and follow the installation screen.

5. After the installation is completed, we can open up the Visual Studio Code. The homepage of Visual Studio Code will look something like this:

6. Now, VS Code itself is really lightweight, and it does not have all the necessary tools to start writing in C# (C-Sharp). That is the reason we need to install this as an extension.

7. To install an extension, click on the last icon located on the left-hand side:

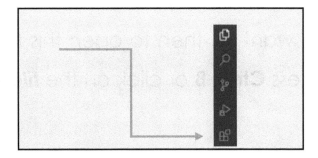

8. Then, Search "C" on the search bar and click the install button. Once the installation is complete, then we are ready to write C# code.

In this extension section, there are handy add-ons, and color themes are available. Some popular are VS Code Icons, Better Syntax, and many more. Now we are going to make a .cs file and open it in Visual studio code:

1.4.2: How to create a C# file using Visual Studio Code:

1. First, make a New Folder on your desktop, and you can name it whatever you want to, then to open this folder inside Visual Studio Code, press **Ctrl + B** or click on the *file's* icon on the left bar:

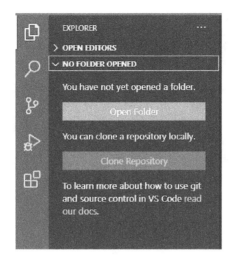

2. After opening the folder in Visual Studio Code, click on the terminal button on the top menu bar, and from there, select "New Terminal" this will open a terminal that should look something like this:

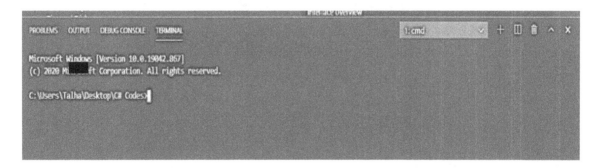

3. A terminal is a command-line program. With these commands, we can give instructions to the computer to do a certain thing like creating files. In this terminal, we need to pass the following command: ***dotnet new console:***

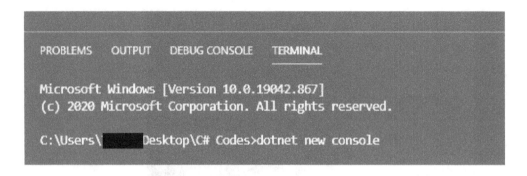

4. When we run the command mentioned earlier, it will create a new project file, and the most important one is the **Program.cs** file, this is what we will use to write our code in.

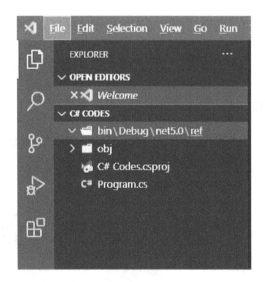

5. Now that our set up for Visual Studio Code is complete, you can now change any setting, like changing the font size by selecting **File > Preferences** or by using the command palette feature of VS Code by **pressing CTRL (Control) + SHIFT + P** on your keyboard and searching for the setting you want to change.

1.4.3: Running the Program.

There are two significant ways to execute the program in Visual Studio Code. In this section, we will a momentary look at the template file **Program.cs** and run the code:

Run code using in build-in terminal:

1. Open New Terminal by clicking on **Terminal** > **New Terminal** on the top menu.

2. Then type the following **.Net** command in the terminal to run the example code: **dotnet run.**

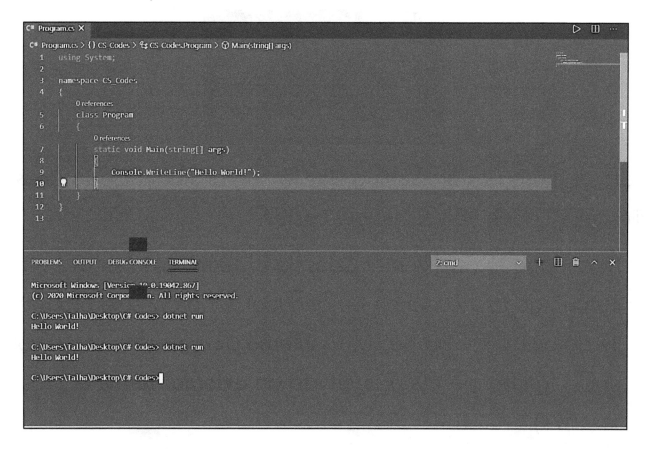

This code shows us output "Hello world", we will discuss all elements of this template file in the next chapter.

Run code in an external terminal:

1. Press **CTRL (Control) + SHIFT + P** to open up the command palette, and then search **Generate**, there you will get the following result:

2. Click on the **.Net Generate Assets for build and Debug.** This will generate two new files in our project directory; **launch** and **tasks,**

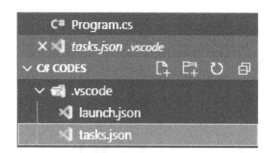

Both of these files are setting files for Visual Studio Code. These files tell VS code how to run our code?

3. To change to an External Console ~~or Terminal to show us~~ the output, go to the launch file and look for a console property. By default, it should be set to **internalConsole. W**e are simply going to change this property to an **external Terminal** (case-sensitive)

```
.vscode > ✗ launch.json > Launch Targets > {} .NET Core Launch (console)
 1   {
 2       "version": "0.2.0",
 3       "configurations": [
 4           {
 5               // Use IntelliSense to find out which attributes exist for C# de
 6               // Use hover for the description of the existing attributes
 7               // For further information visit https://github.com/OmniSharp/om
 8               "name": ".NET Core Launch (console)",
 9               "type": "coreclr",
10               "request": "launch",
11               "preLaunchTask": "build",
12               // If you have changed target frameworks, make sure to update th
13               "program": "${workspaceFolder}/bin/Debug/net5.0/C# Codes.dll",
14               "args": [],
15               "cwd": "${workspaceFolder}",
16               // For more information about the 'console' field, see https://a
17               "console": "externalTerminal",
18               "stopAtEntry": false
19           },
20           {
21               "name": ".NET Core Attach",
22               "type": "coreclr",
23               "request": "attach",
24               "processId": "${command:pickProcess}"
25           }
26       ]
27   }
```

4. Now save this file by pressing **CTRL + S** shortcut key and go back to **Program.cs** then, press **F5** on your keyboard to run your code. This will run your code in an external terminal/console. This may not work as intended, so make sure to add **Console.ReadKey()** after the Hello World line in **Program.cs:**

```
Console.WriteLine("Hello World!");
Console.ReadKey();
```

This will keep the program running until the user presses any button on their keyboard.

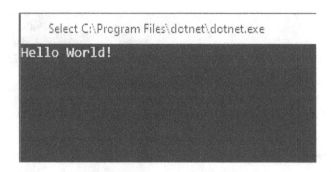

Select C:\Program Files\dotnet\dotnet.exe

Hello World!

1.5: Summary

- A programming language is a computer-generated language that a computer can understand, and there are two types of programming languages: Low-level, High-level.

- C# is a general-purpose, object-oriented programming language that utilizes the Microsoft .NET class library's proven functionality.

- C# can be used to make diverse types of software for every type of operating system.

- Like every High-level language, C# also has a set of rules which must be followed strictly.

Chapter 2: How C# works

2.1: Aspects of a C# file: Hello World Program

In this Section 2.1, We are going to learn about the requirements of a C# file. Please take a look at the code below. It is the same code from the previous section, which was automatically generated as a starting point for us to work with. We can take it as a reference in the coming portions.

```
Using System;

namespace CS_Codes

{

    class Program

    {

        static void Main(string[] args)

        {

        // Next line should print Hello World!

            Console.WriteLine("Hello World!");

            Console.ReadKey();

        }

    }
```

```
}
```

When the code is compiled and is executed, it generates the following output:

```
Hello World!
```

We can divide this code into these parts:

1. Namespace Declaration:

2. A Class

3. Class method

4. Main Method:

5. Statements and Expressions

6. Comments for Readability

Let us look at the various parts of the given program –

- The first line of the program uses **System**; - the *using* keyword specifies that the **System** namespace is included in the program. Generally, a program contains several **using** expressions.

- The following line declares the namespace. The term "**namespace**" refers to a list of classes. The namespace **CS_Code** includes the class **Program**.

- The following line declares a *class* called **Program**, which contains the data and method descriptions that your code utilizes. Generally, classes involve multiple methods. The methods of a class describe its actions. The **Program** class, on the other hand, contains a single method named **Main**.

- The keyword **void** in the Main method's declaration tells the programmer and the compiler what this method should return. For example, it could be a number so that we would write int instead of void.

- Now Explaining the **Main** method, which is where all C# program begins or gets executed. The **Main** method defines what the class does when it is performed, and Main Method is often referred to as the **Driver method** because it runs the code within the class. The static keyword before Main indicates that this method should be accessible without instantiating the class; however, we will discuss this in greater detail in our chapter on classes.

- The compiler ignores the following line **//** (forward slashes), which adds comments to the program. Alternatively, we can also use /* ... */ for multiline comments like this:

```
/*
```

```
This is

a multiline

comment

*/
```

- The Main Method or function defines the behavior of the Main process. WriteLine "Hello, World")

- *WriteLine* is a method of the System namespace's class Console. This statement prompts the screen to show the message *"Hello World"*

- The last line Console.ReadKey(); is for the VS.NET Users. This statement forces the program to wait for a keypress, and it prevents the screen from running and closing quickly when the program is launched from Visual Studio .NET.

2.2: World of Variables and Data Types

Now that you have understood the basics of C# and how it works. In this part of chapter 2, you will get an interpretation of variables and how to name, declare, and initialize them. Additionally, you will learn about the basic operations that can be performed on them. First, we need to understand what a variable actually is.

Variables:

In a C# program, a variable is similar to a container in which a data value can be stored in the computer's memory. A variable's name may be used to refer to the stored value. A variable declaration has this syntax:

For instance, suppose your software requires the user's salary to be stored. To accomplish this, we may call the data **userSalary** and declare the variable **userSalary** as follows:

```
int userSalary;      // stores users salary.
```

The declaration statement specifies the variable's data type first, followed by its name, So the syntax for declaring a variable in C# is:

data-type variable-name;

A variable's data type shows the type of data it will store (for example, whether it is a number or a string of text). The data type in our example is int, which is a short form of integers. Our variable is called **userSalary**.

Naming a Variable:

In C#, a variable's name can only include letters, numbers, or underscores (_). The first character, however, cannot be a number. As a result, your variables can be called **userName,** **user_name**, or **userName2**, but not **2userName**. Additionally, such reserved keywords cannot be used as variable names since they already have pre-defined definitions in C#. These reserved words include **if**, **switch,** and **while**. Each of those will be explained in the upcoming chapters. Finally, variable names are in C# like most other programming languages are also case sensitive. **username** is not equal to **userName**.

When naming a variable in C#, there are two conventions. We may use either **camel case** or **underscores**. Camel casing is a style of writing compound words in which the first letter of each word is capitalized except the first letter of the first word (e.g., **thisIsAVariableName**). This is the convention that will be followed in the remainder of this book. Alternatively, **underscores (_)** are also commonly used to differentiate the terms. Alternatively, you can name your variables as follows: **this_is_a_variable_name.**

Data Types:

In programming, a data type or variable type is a term that defines the kind of value a variable has and the type of operations that can be performed on it without producing an exception. For example, an int is a data type used to represent an integer, while a string is used to describe the text. We can divide data types into three main types:

1. *Numerical*

2. *Text*

3. *Binary*

1. **Numerical**

Numerical data type includes *integer, long, byte, float, double, decimal.*

int and long: **"in"** stands for an integer that is a number with no decimal or fractional parts and holds numbers from **-2,147,483,648 to 2,147,483,647**. Examples include 69, 354, -4, etc. We can also use the **long** keyword to declare an integer number. The difference between a long and an int is of their size and range. A **long** variable can store whole numbers from **-9,223,372,036,854,775,808 to 9,223,372,036,854,775,807**. An int variable is of 4 bytes, and 8 bytes is the size of a variable declared with type long, which means a C# int is 32 bit and long is 64 bit.

The **code example** below declares two variables of type integer and long respectively and then simply prints the assigned value of those variables on screen.

```csharp
using System;

namespace MyApplication

{

    class Program

    {

        static void Main(string[] args)

        {

            int myInt = 5;

            long myLong = 50000000L;    // A long should end wit
h an L


            Console.WriteLine(myInt);

            Console.WriteLine(myLong);

            Console.ReadKey();

        }

    }

}
```

Output:

```
5

50000000
```

byte:

The data type "byte" also relates to integral numbers but with a smaller range of values between **0 and 255**. Usually, we use int rather than byte for integral numbers. However, if you are programming for a computer with limited storage space, you can use byte unless you are sure that the variable's value will not exceed the range 0 to 255. If you declare a byte variable with a number larger than 255, the code won't run, and it will show an error statement. For example, if you need to store a user's age, you should use the byte data form because it is highly improbable that the user's age will ever exceed 255 years.

```
using System;


namespace MyApplication
{
    class Program
    {
```

```
static void Main(string[] args)

{

    byte userAge = 20;    // byte data type's range is 0 to
255

    Console.WriteLine(userAge);

    Console.ReadKey();

    }

  }

}
```

Output:

```
20
```

float, double and decimal:

The term **float** refers to floating-point numbers, which are decimal numbers. such as 15.64, 2.8, and -4.52. *float* can store values between -3.4 x 10 38 and +3.4 x 10 38. It needs 8 bytes of storage and has an estimated precision of 7 digits. This means that if you use *float* to store an amount with ten digits, such as 1.23456789, the value will be rounded to 1.234568. (7 digits). It is important to note that a float value should end with an "F" else compiler will give us an exception:

```
float myNum = 5.7F;

Console.WriteLine(myNum);
```

While **double** is also a floating-point number, it has a much wider range of values. It has a precision of 15 to 16 digits and can store numbers between the range **(+/-)5.0 x 10 -324 and (+/-)1.7 x 10 308.** it is worth noting that you can end the value with a "D" (although not required):

```
double myNum = 19.99D;

Console.WriteLine(myNum);
```

In C#, the **default** floating-point data form is double. In other words, if you write a number like 5.84, C# will automatically treat it as a double.

Decimal is a data type that stores decimal number but has a narrower range than float or double. It does, however, have a significantly higher range of precision, which is about **28-29** digits. When storing non-integral numbers in your program, you should use the decimal data type. Consider the case of writing a financial or a banking application, where accuracy is essential. A floating-point variable can also be used as a scientific number with an **"e,"** which shows the power of 10.

2. Text

Text data type includes *characters, strings.*

char:

The char (character) data type represents a single character or a Unicode symbol. The character must be enclosed in single quotation marks. For instance, **'A'**, **'@'**, and **'o'** etc. In C#, the size of a single character is **two** bytes.

string:

Following the characters, let us examine the string data type. A sequence of characters is stored in a string data form (text). String values must be enclosed in double-quotes (""). The text *"Hello World"* is an example of a string, as strings are groups or sequences of chars, their size is two bytes per character. To declare and initialize a string variable, you write:

```
string message = "Hello World";
```

where message is the variable's name, and "Hello World" is the string it is assigned. Additionally, you can assign an empty string to a variable as follows:

```
string message = "";
```

Finally, we can add two or more strings together using the concatenate symbol **(+)**, and They should be assigned to a variable. For example, we can write:

```
string myName = "Hello World, "+ "my name is Ale";
```

Which is equivalent to `string myName = "Hello World, my name is Ale";`

String: *Methods and Properties*

C# also has plenty of beneficial properties and methods for dealing with strings. To begin, we must understand that, in order to use a property or method, we must use the dot **(.)** operator. To use a property, we type the name of the property following the **dot (.)** To invoke a method, we write its name following the dot operator and followed by a pair of parentheses **()**. Let's take a look at some common properties of a string.

- **Length**

The Length property of a string indicates how many characters the string includes in total. If we want to determine the length of the string **"Hello World"** we will write: **"Hello World". Length;** We'll get the value **11** because "Hello" and "World" both contain **five** characters. When the space between the two terms is used, the total length of the string is 11. **Length** property can be used for validation purposes.

- **Substring()**

Substring() is a method that is used to extract a substring from a longer string. This method needs two arguments. For now, just remember that an argument is the data passed to a method inside the paratheses. We will look at arguments and user-defined methods in upcoming chapters. In **Substring()** method, the first argument instructs the compiler to extract the index of the starting place, and the second requires the compiler to extract the length.

Assume we create a string variable named message and initialize it with the string "Hello World".

string message = "Hello World";

Then, as shown below, we can use the message variable to invoke the Substring() method.

string newMessage = message.Substring(3, 5);

Substring(3, 5) extracts a five-character substring from the message, beginning at index 3. (*which is the fourth letter as indexes always start from 0*). Following that, the resulting Substring is allocated to newMessage.

Thus, newMessage equals **"lo"**. On the other side, the message remains unchanged. It is also still assigned "Hello World"

Code:

```csharp
using System;
namespace MyApplication
{
    class Program
    {

        static void Main(string[] args)
        {
            string message = "Hello World";
            string newMessage = message.Substring(3,4);
            Console.WriteLine(newMessage);
            Console.ReadKey();
        }

    }
}
```

Output:

- **Equals()**

The Equals() method can be used to determine whether two strings are similar. If we have two strings, **firstString = "This is Jami"** and *secondString = "Hell"*, and when we use:

> **firstString.Equals "This is Jami")** this will return true, while:

> **firstString.Equals(secondString)** returns false, since the two strings (*firstString* and *secondString*) are not identical.

For the time being, we are only going to cover Length, Substring, and Equal properties and methods, but there are a lot more pre-defined properties and methods in C#.

3. **Binary or conditional**

The binary data type includes **Bool,** which is short for Boolean and has only two possible values: **true** and **false**. The size of a Bool is only 1 byte. This is a term that is often used in control flow statements.

Data Types Table:

Data Type	Size	Description
int	4 bytes	Stores integers between -2,147,483,648 and 2,147,483,647.
long	8 bytes	Also stores integers from -9,223,372,036,854,775,808 to 9,223,372,036,854,775,807
float	4 bytes	Stores fractional numbers (in decimal format). suitable for storing 6 to 7 decimal digits
double	8 bytes	Stores fractional numbers. Sufficient for storing 15 decimal digits
bool	1 bit	Saves true or false conditions
char	2 bytes	Stores a single character/letter, surrounded by single quotations

string	2 bytes per character	Stores a sequence or combination of characters, surrounded by double quotation marks

Code Showcasing All Major Data types:

```
using System;

namespace MyApplication
{
    class Program
    {
        static void Main(string[] args)
        {
            // Assign Values:
            int myInt = 5F;
            float myFloat = 6.5D;
            double myDouble = 4.16;
```

```csharp
        string message = "Hello World";

        bool isBool = false;


        // Print Values:

        Console.WriteLine(myInt);

        Console.WriteLine(myFloat);

        Console.WriteLine(myDouble);

        Console.WriteLine(message);

        Console.WriteLine(isBool);


        Console.ReadKey();
    }

}


}
```

Output:

```
5
6.5
4.16
Hello World
False
```

2.3: The Assignment Symbol

The **=** symbol or sign has a different meaning in programming than it does in mathematics. The = sign is referred to as an **assignment** sign in programming. Unlike in mathematics, it is referred to as **equal to sign**. This indicates that the value on the right of the = sign is assigned to the left variable. For example, *age* *= 5*. The statements x = y and y = x has vastly different definitions in programming. This is not what we learned in mathematics; rather, we learned that x and y would most likely be different quantities. Assume we have two variables, x, and y,

with **x = 6** and **y = 12.**

If we write **x = y;**

This is applicable in programming. This statement indicates that the value of y is being assigned to x. It is appropriate to assign the value of one variable to another. In our example, we've changed the value of **x** to **12** while leaving the value of y unchanged. In other words, **x** and **y** are now **equal** to **12**. Now suppose we restore the values of x and y to their original values:

x = 6 and y = 12;

If you now write **y = x;**

This indicates that you are assigning the value of **x** to **y**, x = y and y = x both are equivalent mathematically. This is not the case in programming. Here, y is set to 12 while x remains unchanged. In other terms, x equals six, and y equals six. In the subsequent section, we will also see combinations of assignment signs with other operators in C#.

2.4: Operators in C#

Operators are the building blocks of every programming language. As a result, without the use of operators, the functionality of the C# language is incomplete. Operators enable us to perform several types of operations on variables. In C#, operators are classified according to their functionality:

- Arithmetical Operators

- Relational Operators

- Logical Operators

- Bitwise Operators

- Assignment Operators (continued)

- Conditional Operator

We can also classify Operators in C# based on the number of operands or variables:

- **Unary Operator:** An operator that operates with only one operand.

- **Binary Operator:** An operator that operates on two operands.

- **Ternary Operator:** An operator that operates with three operands.

After learning about all of the operators mentioned above, we will use them one by one in a C# code.

Arithmetic Operators

These are used to carry out arithmetic and mathematical operations on variables. These are the Binary Operators that fall into this category:

- **Addition:** The "+" operator joins two variables together. For instance, x + y.

- **Subtraction:** The "-" operator is used to deduct two variables. For instance, a - b.

- **Multiplication:** The " * " is called multiplication operator, is used to find the product of two variables. For instance, x * y.

- **Division:** The "/" operator divides the first variables by the second variables. As an example, consider a / b.

- **Modulus:** When the first operand or variable is divided by the second, the "%" operator returns the remainder. For instance, x % y.

Unary Operators that come under arithmetic operators include the following:

1. The **++** operator is used to increment an integer's value. When placed earlier than the variable name (also known as the **pre-increment** operator), the variable's value is immediately incremented. For instance, **++x.**

2. And when it is put after the variable name (also known as the **post-increment** operator), its value is stored temporarily before this statement is executed and then modified before the following information is performed. For instance, **x++.**

3. The **'--'** operator is used to decrement an integer's value. When preceding the variable name (also known as the **pre-decrement** operator), the value of the variable is decremented immediately. For instance, **--x.**

4. And when it is put after the variable name (also known as the **post-decrement** operator), its value is stored temporarily before it is executed and then modified before the following statement is executed. For instance, **x--**. By default, **++** and -- increment and decrement the value by **1**.

Code Example (Arithmetic and Unary):

```
using System;

namespace ArithmeticAndUnary

{

    class myProgram

    {


        // Main Function

        static void Main(string[] args)

        {


            int result;

            int x = 10, y = 5;
```

```csharp
Console.WriteLine("\tARITHMETIC Operators: ");


    // Addition

    result = (x + y);

    Console.WriteLine("Addition Operator: " + result);


    // Subtraction

    result = (x - y);

    Console.WriteLine("Subtraction Operator: " + result
);


    // Multiplication

    result = (x * y);

    Console.WriteLine("Multiplication Operator: "+ resul
t);


    // Division

    result = (x / y);

    Console.WriteLine("Division Operator: " + result);
```

```csharp
// Modulo

result = (x % y);

Console.WriteLine("Modulo Operator: " + result);




/* UNARY */

Console.WriteLine("\v\tUNARY Operators: ");

// post-increment example:

// result is assigned 10 only,

// x is not updated yet

result = x++;


 //x becomes 11 now

Console.WriteLine("X is {0} and result is {1}", x, result
);


// post-decrement example:
```

```csharp
        // result is assigned 11 only, x is not updated yet

        result = x--;


        //x becomes 10 now

        Console.WriteLine("X is {0} and result
is {1}", x, result);




        // pre-increment example:

        // result is assigned 11 now since y

        // is updated here itself

        result = ++y;


        // a and res have same values = 11

        Console.WriteLine("Y is {0} and result
is {1}", y, result);



        // pre-decrement example:

        // result is assigned 10 only since
```

```
        // y is updated here itself

        result = --y;


        // y and result have same values = 10

        Console.WriteLine("Y is {0} and result
is {1}",y, result);

        Console.ReadKey();



    }

  }

}
```

Output:

```
          ARITHMETIC Operators:
Addition Operator: 15
Subtraction Operator: 5
Multiplication Operator: 50
Division Operator: 2
Modulo Operator: 0

          UNARY Operators:
X is 11 and res is 10
X is 10 and res is 11
Y is 6 and res is 6
Y is 5 and res is 5
```

- **Relational Operators**

Two values are compared using relational operators. Let check them through them one by one:

1. The '=' (Equal To) operator determines if two variables are equal. If this is the case, it returns true. Otherwise, false is returned. For instance, **7 == 7** will return **true**.

2. The **'!'** (Not Equal To) operator determines whether the two variables are equal. If the variables are not equal, it returns **true**. Otherwise, **false** is returned. It is the Boolean complement(opposite) to the operator **'=='**. For instance, **7! = 7** returns **false**.

3. The operator **">"** (Greater Than) verifies that the first variable is greater than the second variable. If this is the case, it returns **true**. Otherwise, **false** is returned. For instance, **7 > 4** returns **true**.

4. The operator **"<"** "(Less Than) verifies that the first operand or variable is less than the second variable. If this is the case, it returns **true**. Otherwise, false is returned. For instance, **65 < 8** returns **false**.

5. The **'>='** (Greater Than Equal To) operator determines if the first variable is greater than or equal to the second variable. If this

is the case, it returns **true**. Otherwise, **false** is returned. For instance, **5 >= 5** returns true.

6. The **'<='** (Less Than Equal To) operator determines if the first variable is less than or equal to the second variable. If this is the case, it returns **true**. Otherwise, **false** is returned. For instance, **5 <= 5** returns true as well. Both **'>='** and **'<='** are especially useful in loops.

- **Logical Operators**

These operators are used to combine two or more conditions/constraints or complement the initial condition assessment. They are as follows:

1. The **logical AND '&&'** operator returns true when all conditions are met. Otherwise, false is returned. For example, when both a and b are true, a && b returns true (i.e., non-zero).

2. The **logical OR '||'** operator returns true if one (or both) of the conditions are fulfilled. Otherwise, false is returned. For instance, a || b returns true if one of the arguments a or b is valid (i.e., non-zero). Naturally, it produces true if and only if both a and b are true.

3. **NOT logical operator:** The **'!'** operator returns true when the condition in consideration is not met. Otherwise, false is

returned. For instance, !**a** gives true if **a** is false, that is when a = 0. Logical operators are most commonly used in conditional statements.

Code Example (relational and logical):

```
using System;

namespace RealtionalAndLogical

{

    class myProgram

    {


        // Main Function

        static void Main(string[] args)

        {



            int x = 10, y = 5;                    // for rational operators

            bool a = true, b = false, result;    // for logical operators
```

```csharp
            Console.WriteLine("\v\tRealtional Operators: ");


        // Equal to Operator

        result = (x == y);

        Console.WriteLine("Equal to Operator: " + result);


        // Greater than Operator

        result = (x > y);

        Console.WriteLine("Greater than Operator: " + resu
lt);


        // Less than Operator

        result = (x < y);

        Console.WriteLine("Less than Operator: " + result);


        // Greater than Equal to Operator

        result = (x >= y);

        Console.WriteLine("Greater than or Equal to: "+ res
ult);
```

```csharp
// Less than Equal to Operator

result = (x <= y);

Console.WriteLine("Lesser than or Equal to: "+ result
);

// Not Equal To Operator

result = (x != y);

Console.WriteLine("Not Equal to Operator: " + resul
t);


Console.WriteLine("\v\tLogical Operators: ");


// AND operator

result = a && b;

Console.WriteLine("AND Operator: " + result);


// OR operator

result = a || b;
```

```
            Console.WriteLine("OR Operator: " + result);



        // NOT operator

        result = !a;

        Console.WriteLine("NOT Operator: " + result);




        }

    }

}
```

Output:

```
        Realtional Operators:
Equal to Operator: False
Greater than Operator: True
Less than Operator: False
Greater than or Equal to: True
Lesser than or Equal to: False
Not Equal to Operator: True

        Logical Operators:
AND Operator: False
OR Operator: True
NOT Operator: False
```

Bitwise Operators

There are six bitwise operators in C# that operate at the bit level or perform bit by bit operations. The bitwise operators are as follows:

1. **& (bitwise AND):** takes two variables and performs **AND** on each bit of the two variables. **AND** returns **1** only if both variables are **1**.

2. **| (bitwise OR):** takes two variables or operands and performs **OR** on each bit of the two variables. **OR** returns **1** if one of the two bits is **one** or both bits are one.

3. **^ (bitwise XOR):** Takes two operands or variables and performs XOR on each bit of the two variables. If the two bits are not identical, the result of XOR is **1**.

4. **<< (left shift):** Takes two numbers. Left changes the bits in the first operand or variable and specifies the number of places to shift in the second variable.

5. **>> (Right shift):** Takes two numbers, right changes the bits of the first variable, and the number of places to move is determined by the second variable.

Code Example (Bitwise operators):

```
using System;
```

```csharp
namespace BitwiseOperators
{
    class myProgram
    {
        // Main Function
        static void Main(string[] args)
        {

            int x = 10, y = 5, result;


            Console.WriteLine("\v\tBITWISE Operator");

                // Bitwise AND Operator
                result = x & y;
                Console.WriteLine("Bitwise AND: " + result);

                // Bitwise OR Operator
                result = x | y;
```

```csharp
        Console.WriteLine("Bitwise OR: " + result);


        // Bitwise XOR Operator

        result = x ^ y;

        Console.WriteLine("Bitwise XOR: " + result);


        // Bitwise AND Operator

        result = ~x;

        Console.WriteLine("Bitwise Complement: " + result);


        // Bitwise LEFT SHIFT Operator

        result = x << 2;

        Console.WriteLine("Bitwise Left Shift: " + result);


        // Bitwise RIGHT SHIFT Operator

        result = x >> 2;

        Console.WriteLine("Bitwise Right Shift: " + result);


    }
```

```
        }

    }
```

Output:

```
              BITWISE Operator
Bitwise AND: 0
Bitwise OR: 15
Bitwise XOR: 15
Bitwise Complement: -11
Bitwise Left Shift: 40
Bitwise Right Shift: 2
```

- **Assignment Operators**

We already covered the primary assignment sign **"="** in section 2.3 of this chapter. Now, we are going to learn about several types of assignment operators. First, let's review the simple **"="** operator. This operator is used to assign variables their values. The left operand or variable of the assignment operator is a variable, and the right operand is a value. The weight on the right should be of the same data type as the attribute on the left side. Otherwise, the compiler would reject it. Different assignment operators are shown below:

1. **"+=" (Add Assignment):** This operator is a combination of the operators **"+"** and **"="**. This operator starts with the value on the left and applies the current value.

2. **"-=" (Subtract Assignment):** This operator is a mixture of the operators "-" and "=". This operator subtracts the current value of the left variable from the right value and then assigns the result to the left variable.

3. **"*=" (Multiply Assignment):** This operator is a mixture of **the** '*' and '=' operators. This operator assigns the result to the variable on the left after multiplying the existing value of the variable on the left by the value on the right.

4. **"/=" (Division Assignment):** This operator is a mixture of the operators "/" and "=". This operator divides the current value of the left variable by the right variable's value and then assigns the result to the left variable.

5. **"%=" (Modulus Assignment):** This operator is a mixture of the "%" and the "=" operators. This operator modulo the current value of the left variable by the right value or variable and then assigns the result to the left variable.

6. **"<<=" (Left Shift Assignment):** This operator is a mixture of the operators "<< "and '='. This operator left shifts the current value of the left variable by the right value and then assigns the result to the left variable.

7. **">>=" (Right Shift Assignment):** This operator is a variation of the operators **">>"** and **"="**. This operator right shifts the current value of the leftmost variable by the right value and then assigns the result to the left variable.

8. **"&=" (Bitwise AND Assignment):** This operator is a mixture of the operators **"&"** and **"="**. Firstly, this operator "Bitwise AND" the existing value of the variable on the left with the value on the right before assigning the result to the variable on the left.

9. **"|=" (Bitwise Inclusive OR):** This operator is a combination of the operators **"|"** and **"="**. this operator "Bitwise Inclusive OR" the present value of the variable on the left to the value on the right and then assigns the result to the variable on the left.

10. **"^=" (Bitwise Exclusive OR):** This operator is a combination of the **"^"** and the **"="** operators. This operator assigns the result to the variable on the left after doing the "Bitwise Exclusive OR" operation on the present value of the variable on the left by the value on the right.

Code Example (Assignment operators):

```
using System;

namespace AssignmentOperators

{
```

```csharp
class myProgram

{


    // Main Function

    static void Main(string[] args)

    {

        // initialize variable x

        // using Simple Assignment

        // Operator "="

        int x = 15;


        Console.WriteLine("\v\assignment Operators: ");


        // it means x = x + 10

        x += 10;

        Console.WriteLine("Add Assignment Operator: " + x
);


        // initialize variable x again
```

```csharp
x = 20;

// it means x = x - 5

x -= 5;

Console.WriteLine("Subtract Assignment Operator: " + x);

// initialize variable x again

x = 15;

// it means x = x * 5

x *= 5;

Console.WriteLine("Multiply Assignment Operator: " + x);

// initialize variable x again

x = 25;

// it means x = x / 5
```

```csharp
x /= 5;
Console.WriteLine("Division Assignment Operator: " + x);


// initialize variable x again
x = 36;


// it means x = x % 5
x %= 5;
Console.WriteLine("Modulo Assignment Operator: " + x);


// initialize variable x again
x = 8;


// it means x = x << 2
x <<= 2;
Console.WriteLine("Left Shift Assignment Operator: " + x);
```

```csharp
// initialize variable x again

x = 8;


// it means x = x >> 2

x >>= 2;

Console.WriteLine("Right Shift Assignment Operator: " + x);


// initialize variable x again

x = 12;


// it means x = x >> 4

x &= 4;

Console.WriteLine("Bitwise AND Assignment Operator: " + x);


// initialize variable x again

x = 12;
```

```csharp
        // it means x = x >> 4

        x ^= 4;

        Console.WriteLine("Bitwise Exclusive OR Assignmen
t Operator: " + x);


        // initialize variable x again

        x = 12;

        // it means x = x >> 4

        x |= 4;

        Console.WriteLine("Bitwise Inclusive OR Assignment
Operator: " + x);
    }

  }
}
```

Output:

```
          ASSIGNMENT Operators:
Add Assignment Operator: 25
Subtract Assignment Operator: 15
Multiply Assignment Operator: 75
Division Assignment Operator: 5
Modulo Assignment Operator: 1
Left Shift Assignment Operator: 32
Right Shift Assignment Operator: 2
Bitwise AND Assignment Operator: 4
Bitwise Exclusive OR Assignment Operator: 8
Bitwise Inclusive OR Assignment Operator: 12
```

2.5: Summary

In this chapter, we learned about how C# works, what are the requirements of a C# script? After that, we covered various Data Types available to us in C#. We learned about all the basic operators that can be used to perform arithmetical, logical, or relational calculations.

Chapter 3: Practical Uses

In this chapter, we are going to increase our understanding of C# by taking a look at working with user input and conditional statements, and after understanding these core concepts, we will program a basic calculator, but before doing that, let us look at some practical applications, which can be developed using C#. It is a flexible programming language that can be used in a variety of situations. We already discussed the uses of C# very briefly, but that was just a glimpse of what can be made with C#.

- C#, as stated before, is a very flexible language that can be used for making simple command-line programs for learning purposes. But with lots of frameworks and APIs (application programming interface), we can make any type of software or a game.

- Games are made either using a graphics library or software toolkit called a game engine. One of the most popular game engines in game development, called **unity3d**, utilizes **C#** as its programming language. Unity provides Its own scripting **API** with custom data types, functions, and a set of tools to help developers make games. All classes in unity are derived from a base class called MonoBehaviour.

- **ASP.NET** is an open-source framework for making server-side web applications. ASP.NET also comes with pre-defined functions.

- **.NET** framework is used for many things such as gaming, making applications. The best part of .Net is its easy integration across different platforms (cross-platform support) .Net also has a large community that helps regarding the issues and has many web forums to ask any type of question regarding .Net. It also provides excellent scalability for developing small and large applications.

3.1: Printing Output

As previously mentioned, **Console.WriteLine()** is used to print (output) values. Now we'll read the data entered by the user using **Console.ReadLine().** Take a look at the code example given below:

```
using System;

namespace InputAndOutput

{

    class myProgram

    {
```

```csharp
// Main Function

static void Main(string[] args)

{


    Console.WriteLine("Hello World");

    Console.Write("Prints");

    Console.Write(" on the same Line");

    Console.ReadKey();



    }

  }

}
```

Output:

```
Hello World
Prints on the same Line
```

As you can see, both **Console.WriteLine()** and **Console.Write()** are used for printing values. The only difference is that **Write()** method does not skip lines (whitespace), and on the other hand **WriteLine()** method after printing an output then moves to the next line. We can also easily print values of variables using both of the methods mentioned above, for example:

```csharp
using System;
namespace InputAndOutput
{
    class myProgram
    {

        // Main Function
        static void Main(string[] args)
        {

            int userAge = 25;

            Console.WriteLine("Age: " + userAge);
            Console.ReadKey();

        }

    }
```

```
}
```

Output:

```
Age: 25
```

So, we can easily print values of variables. Now we will make our program dynamic by giving the user the ability to enter their age and save the data in the **userAge** variable.

3.2: User Input

The easiest way to obtain user input in C# is to use the Console class's **ReadLine()** method. However, the functions **Read()** and **ReadKey()** are alternatives for obtaining user input. They are contained in the Console class.

```
using System;

namespace Input

{

    class myProgram

    {

        public static void Main(string[] args)

        {
```

```
        string myString;

        Console.Write("Enter a string: ");

        myString = Console.ReadLine();

        Console.WriteLine("You entered '{0}':", myString);

         Console.ReadKey();

      }

    }

}
```

Output:

```
Enter a string: hello
You entered 'hello':
```

When the above program is executed, it prompts the user to enter a string, and when the user enters a string, it gets saved in the **myString,** and after that, it is simply printed on the screen.

Now here you might have noticed '{0}' in the ***Console.WriteLine()*** this is another way of saying:

```
    Console.WriteLine("You entered: " + myString);
```

{0} is a placeholder for myString as there is only one variable to print, so there is only one placeholder.

Difference between ReadLine(), Read() and ReadKey() method:

- **ReadLine()** reads the following input from the regular input stream. It returns the same string.

- The **Read()** method extracts the following character from the input stream's normal input. It returns the character's ASCII value.

- The **ReadKey()** method retrieves the next key pressed by the user. This is typically used to keep the screen in place before the user presses a key.

```
using System;

namespace Input

{

    class myProgram

    {

        public static void Main(string[] args)

        {

            int testInput;


            Console.WriteLine("Press any key to continue");

            Console.ReadKey();

            Console.WriteLine();
```

```csharp
        Console.Write("Input using Read(): ");

        testInput = Console.Read();                    // returns int

        Console.WriteLine("\vAscii Value = {0}", testInput);

    }

  }

}
```

Output:

```
Press any key to continue
o
Input using Read(): a
                      Ascii Value = 97
```

This example should demonstrate how the **ReadKey()** and **Read()** methods operate. When ReadKey() is used, the key is shown on the screen immediately after it is pressed. When **Read()** is used, the entire line is read, but only the ASCII value of the first character is returned. As a result, 97 (a's ASCII value) is written.

Entering Numeric Values

In **C#**, reading a character or string is straightforward. All that is required is to call the corresponding methods as specified. However, interpreting numeric values in C# can be a little tricky.

We'll continue to use the **ReadLine()** method that we used to obtain string values. However, since the **ReadLine()** method accepts string input, it must be converted to an integer or floating-point form. One straightforward way for converting our input is to use the **Convert** class's methods, which is also classified as a member of the System namespace.

The **ToInt32()** method is used to convert a string to an integer. For example, consider the *string userInput = Console.ReadLine();*

and suppose that the user enters **15** into userInput, userInput will equal "**15**" (which is a string, not an integer, due to the double quotes). We can then use:

int newUserInput = Convert.ToInt32(userInput);

To convert the string to the integer 15 and assign it to an int variable using the *int newUserInput = Convert.ToInt32(userInput);* method. On this new int variable, we can now execute standard mathematical operations.

Apart from converting a string to an integer, we can also use the *ToDecimal()*, *ToSingle()*, and *ToDouble()* methods to convert a string to a **decimal**, **float**, or **double**.

```
using System;
```

```csharp
namespace UserInput
{
    class myProgram
    {
        public static void Main(string[] args)
        {
            string userInput;

            int intVal;

            double doubleVal;


            Console.Write("Enter integer value: ");

            userInput = Console.ReadLine();

            /* Converts to integer type */

            intVal = Convert.ToInt32(userInput);

            Console.WriteLine("You entered {0}",intVal);


            Console.Write("Enter double value: ");

            userInput = Console.ReadLine();

            /* Converts to double type */
```

```
        doubleVal = Convert.ToDouble(userInput);

        Console.WriteLine("You entered {0}",doubleVal);

    }

}

}
```

Output:

```
Enter integer value: 351
You entered 351
Enter double value: 51.61
You entered 51.61
```

Now we know how to work with user input and convert it to our desired data type using the methods from the Convert class, which is contained inside the system namespace. Let's now learn about flow control with if, else if, else, and switch statements.

3.3 Flow Control: Conditional Statements

Flow control is the sequence in which function calls, instructions, and statements are performed or evaluated during the execution of a program. Numerous programming languages provide what are known as control flow statements, which specify which section of code is executed at any point in time. An if/else statement is an example of a control flow statement.

if, if...else, else.

The if statement is a common control flow statement. It enables the program to determine whether a specified condition is met and to take appropriate action based on the outcome of the assessment. The syntax of an if statement in C# is as follows.

```
1. if (//condition first is true or false)

2. {

3. // do Task a

4. }

5. else if (//condition first is true or false)

6. {

7. // do Task B

8. }

9. else if (//condition second is true or false)

10.     {

11.     // do Task C

12.     }

13.     else

14.     {

15.     // do Task E or default choice
```

```
16.    }
```

Line 1 evaluates the initial state. If the condition is met, the following pair of curly braces (lines 2 to 4) will be performed. The remainder of the if sentence (lines 5–16) will be omitted.

Suppose the first condition is not met. The else if statements that follow can be used to conduct additional tests (lines 5 to 12). Other else if comments are permissible. Finally, you can execute code using the else statement (lines 13 to 16). If none of the preceding tests are satisfied, then the last else statement is completed, which is also used to handle incorrect input. Now, let's use our recent understanding of the first conditional statement if/else if/else in a practical program.

```
using System;


namespace Conditionals

{

    class myProgram

    {

        public static void Main(string[] args)

        {
```

```csharp
//input an integer number and check whether
//it is postive, negative or zero
int number;

Console.Write("Enter an integer number: ");
number = Convert.ToInt32(Console.ReadLine());

//checking conditions
if (number > 0)
    Console.WriteLine("{0} is a positive number", number);
else if (number < 0)
    Console.WriteLine("{0} is a negative number", number);
else
    Console.WriteLine("{0} was entered", number);

//hit ENTER to exit the program
Console.ReadLine();
```

```
        }

    }

}
```

In the preceding program, we requested that the user insert an integer, and first, the string input is converted to int data type, and after that, we check if the number variable is greater than 0, which means the integer, which means that the user entered is positive if that's not true, then the compiler skips the first if statement and runs the else if statement to check if the number entered by the user is negative if it is not negative then the else statement is executed. You may have observed that we did not use curly braces to enclose the statement. This is because curly braces are optional when running a single statement.

Output:

```
Enter an integer number: 48
48 is a positive number
```

or

```
Enter an integer number: -4
-4 is a negative number
```

or

```
Enter an integer number: 0
0 was entered
```

Nested if...else Statement

Inside one if...else statement block, another if...else statement is can also exist. This concept is referred to as **nested if...else**. The syntax of a nested if...else statement is as follows:

```
if (//test-condition)

{

    if (//nested-expression-1)

    {

        // code to be executed

    }

    else

    {

        // code to be executed

    }

}

else

{

    if (//nested-expression-2)

    {
```

```
            // code to be executed

        }

    else

    {

        // code to be executed

    }

}
```

Generally, we use nested if statements when we need to evaluate one condition followed by another. If the exterior if statement returns true, it enters the body of the nested if statement to verify the internal if statement.

For better understanding, check out the code given below:

```
using System;

namespace Conditional

{

    class Nested

    {

        public static void Main(string[] args)

        {
```

```csharp
int first, second, third;

Console.Write("Enter first number: ");
first = Convert.ToInt32(Console.ReadLine());

Console.Write("Enter second number: ");
second = Convert.ToInt32(Console.ReadLine());

Console.Write("Enter third number: ");
third = Convert.ToInt32(Console.ReadLine());

if (first > second)
{
    if (first > third)
    {
        Console.WriteLine("{0} is the largest number", first);
    }
    else
```

```csharp
                {
                        Console.WriteLine("{0} is the largest number", thir
d);
                }
        }
        else
        {
        if (second > third)
        {
                Console.WriteLine("{0} is the largest number", se
cond);
        }
        else
        {
                Console.WriteLine("{0} is the largest number", thir
d);
        }
        }
        // forces the screen stay on until a key is pressed
```

```
        Console.Readkey();

    }

  }

}
```

Output:

```
Enter first number: 461
Enter second number: 15
Enter third number: 649
649 is the largest number
```

Inline If:

An inline if statement is a more condensed version of an if statement that is extremely useful when you want to assign a value to a variable based on the outcome of a situation. The syntax is as follows:

```
// circumstance? value if the circumstance is true : value if the condition is false;
```

For example, the statement **9 > 6? 10: 5;** returns the value **10** because three is greater than two (i.e., the condition three > two is true).

After that, this value can be assigned to a variable.

If we write int **myNum = 9 > 6? 10: 5**, the value of **myNum** will be set to **10**.

Switch Statement

In C#, the switch statement can be used in place of the if...else if statement. The benefit of switch over if...else if statements are that the code would appear much simpler and more readable. The switch statement has the following syntax:

```
switch (variable/expression)

{

    case caseOne:

    // Statements executed if expression(or variable) =
caseOne

        break;

    case caseTwo:

    // Statements executed if expression(or variable) =
caseTwo

        break;


    default:

        // Statements executed if no case matches

        break

}
```

When using a switch expression, you can have as many cases as you want. The default case is an optional one that is carried out when none of the previous cases are selected or executed.

However, a disadvantage of the switch statement over, if-else, is that it executes all following arguments before the switch block is concluded when a matching value is detected. To prevent this, we end each case with a break statement. Completing the switch statement's execution makes the break statement prevent the program from executing non-matching statements. One everyday use of switch statements is to create menus where the user can select an option **(any case from switch statement).**

3.4: Calculator using Switch in C#:

```
using System;


namespace Conditionals

{

    class myCalculator

    {

        public static void Main(string[] args)

        {
```

```csharp
char ch;

double firstNum, secondNum, result;


Console.Write("Enter first number: ");

firstNum = Convert.ToDouble(Console.ReadLine());


Console.Write("Enter second number: ");

secondNum = Convert.ToDouble(Console.ReadLine(
));


Console.Write("Enter operator ( +, -, *, /, %): ");

ch = Convert.ToChar(Console.ReadLine());


switch(ch)

{

    case '+':

        result = firstNum + secondNum;

        Console.WriteLine("{0} + {1} = {2}", firstNum, seco
ndNum, result);
```

```
        break;


    case '-':

    result = firstNum - secondNum;

    Console.WriteLine("{0} - {1} = {2}", firstNum, secon
dNum, result);

        break;


    case '*':

    result = firstNum * secondNum;

    Console.WriteLine("{0} * {1} = {2}", firstNum, seco
ndNum, result);

        break;


    case '/':

    result = firstNum / secondNum;

    Console.WriteLine("{0} / {1} = {2}", firstNum, seco
ndNum, result);

        break;
```

```csharp
            case '%':

                result = firstNum % secondNum;

                Console.WriteLine("{0} % {1} = {2}", firstNum, seco
ndNum, result);

                break;


            default:

                Console.WriteLine("Invalid Operator!!");

                break;


        }

    }

}

}
```

Output:

```
Enter first number: 14
Enter second number: 2
Enter operator ( +, -, *, /, %): +
14 + 2 = 16
```

```
Enter first number: 14
Enter second number: 2
Enter operator ( +, -, *, /, %): -
14 - 2 = 12
```

```
Enter first number: 14
Enter second number: 2
Enter operator ( +, -, *, /, %): *
14 * 2 = 28
```

```
Enter first number: 14
Enter second number: 2
Enter operator ( +, -, *, /, %): /
14 / 2 = 7
```

```
Enter first number: 14
Enter second number: 3
Enter operator ( +, -, *, /, %): %
14 % 3 = 2
```

3.5: Summary

- For printing values, we use **Console.Write()** or **Console.WriteLine()**

- For user input, we use **Console.ReadLine()** or **Console.Read()**, but these take input in String data type only, but we can easily convert this input into our desired data type by using Convert class's method, which is a member of the System namespace.

- In this chapter, we also learned about two types of conditional statements (**if..else- if..else** and **switch**)

Chapter 4: Make a Complete Program

In this chapter, we will continue working with flow control statements by learning about looping in programming. We will make our calculator more interactive by integrating loops in the same code.

4.1: Flow Control: Loops

Loops are a fundamental and compelling principle in programming. A loop is an instruction that is repeated until a given condition is met in a computer program. A loop structure is a question-answering structure. If the question requires a response, the response is carried out. In this section, we will learn about For, While/ Do-while, and foreach loop.

While Loop:

As the name implies, a while loop repeatedly executes instructions inside the loop as long as a specified condition is true. A while statement is structured as follows:

```
while (test)

{

    // body of a while loop

}
```

Working of a while loop in C#:

1. A while loop in C# is composed of a test expression.

2. If the test-expression evaluates to true:

   - the while loop's statements are executed.

   - Following the execution, the test statement is re-evaluated.

3. The while loop ends if the test statement evaluates to false.

The sum of the first ten natural numbers is computed by this program.

```csharp
using System;

namespace Loops
{
    class WhileLoop
    {
        public static void Main(string[] args)
        {
            int i = 1, sum = 0;
```

```
    while (i <= 10)

    {

        // Adds i + i, and saves in sum

        sum += i;

        // increments i until the condition is met

        i++;

    }

    // prints

    Console.WriteLine("Sum of first 10 natural numbers is
{0}", sum);

    }

    }

}
```

Output:

```
Sum of first 10 natural numbers 55
```

At the start, the value of the sum variable is set to 0. Each iteration updates the value of sum to **sum + i** and increments the value of **i** by **1**. When i equals 11, the test expression **i <= 10** returns false, and the loop ends.

do-while Loop:

A do-while loop is created using the do and while keywords. Although it is similar to a while loop, there is a significant difference between the two. In a While loop, the code is only executed if the test condition is met. The test condition is checked after the code inside the do body is performed in a do-while loop. This ensures that regardless of the situation, the **do-while loop** is at least completed one time. The syntax is as follows:

```
do
{
    // body of a do-while loop
}
while (test-expression);
```

Working of a do-while loop in C#:

1. At first, the body of the do...while loop is executed.

2. Then the evaluation of the test expression occurs.

3. The loop's body is executed if the test expression is true.

4. When the test expression evaluates to false, the do...while loop ends.

```
using System;
```

```csharp
namespace Loops
{
    class DoWhileLoop
    {
        public static void Main(string[] args)
        {
            int x = 6;
            do
            {
                // The line will be printed evenif the condition is false
                Console.WriteLine("Do While Loop is always executed once!");
                x++;
            }
            while (x > 20);
        }
    }
}
```

for Loop:

The **for** loop repeatedly executes a block of code until the test condition no longer remains true. It's called for loop because **for** keyword is required to create a looping start-point, the syntax of a for loop is:

```
for (initialization; condition; iterator)
{

    // body of for loop

}
```

Working of a for loop in C#:

1. Three statements comprise the C# for loop: initialization, condition, and iterator.

2. Initialization is executed only once. Typically, the variable is declared and initialized here.

3. The condition is then assessed. The condition is a Boolean expression, which means that it evaluates to true or false.

4. **If the condition is true or it is met:**

   - The iterator statement is then executed, which usually modifies the initialized variable's value.

   - The condition is tested once more.

- The procedure is repeated until the condition is determined to be incorrect.

- The for loop terminates if the condition is evaluated to be incorrect.

The code below lets the user enter a number, and then it prints the multiplication table until **10** of the number entered by the user.

```csharp
using System;

namespace Loops
{
    class ForLoop
    {
        public static void Main(string[] args)
        {
            int limit = 10, myNum, product = 0;

            Console.Write("Enter a number: ");
            myNum = Convert.ToInt32(Console.ReadLine());
```

```csharp
for (int i = 1; i <= limit; i++)

{


    product = myNum * i;

    Console.WriteLine("{1} x {0} = {2}", i, myNum, product);

}



        }

    }

}
```

Output:

```
Enter a number: 3
3 x 1 = 3
3 x 2 = 6
3 x 3 = 9
3 x 4 = 12
3 x 5 = 15
3 x 6 = 18
3 x 7 = 21
3 x 8 = 24
3 x 9 = 27
3 x 10 = 30
```

foreach Loop:

C# provides an easier-to-use, and more readable alternative to the for loop called the foreach loop when it comes to iterating through the elements of arrays and collections. The foreach loop, as the name implies, iterates through each item. We will cover arrays in detail in the next chapter. For now, remember that arrays are collections of variables with the same data type. Syntax of a foreach loop is:

```
foreach (element in iterable-item)
{
    // body of foreach loop
}
```

Now let's make our make calculator program more interactive which we made in section 3.4. We will add Do while loop in our code and ask the user if they want to do more calculations.

4.2: Dynamic Calculator

```
using System;

namespace Conditionals
{
```

```csharp
class myCalculator
{
    public static void Main(string[] args)
    {
        char ch;
        double firstNum, secondNum, result;
        string restart = " ";

        do
        {
            Console.Write("Enter first number: ");
            firstNum = Convert.ToDouble(Console.ReadLine());

            Console.Write("Enter second number: ");
            secondNum = Convert.ToDouble(Console.ReadLine());

            Console.Write("Enter operator ( +, -, *, /, %): ");
            ch = Convert.ToChar(Console.ReadLine());
```

```csharp
        switch(ch)

        {

            case '+':

                result = firstNum + secondNum;

                Console.WriteLine("{0} + {1} = {2}", firstNum, se
condNum, result);

                Console.Write("Do you want to do more calc
ulations?(Yes/No): ");

                restart = Console.ReadLine();

                break;


            case '-':

                result = firstNum - secondNum;

                Console.WriteLine("{0} - {1} = {2}", firstNum, sec
ondNum, result);

                Console.Write("Do you want to do more calc
ulations?(Yes/No): ");

                restart = Console.ReadLine();
```

```csharp
                break;


        case '*':

            result = firstNum * secondNum;

            Console.WriteLine("{0} * {1} = {2}", firstNum, sec
ondNum, result);

            Console.Write("Do you want to do more calc
ulations?(Yes/No): ");

            restart = Console.ReadLine();

            break;


        case '/':

            result = firstNum / secondNum;

            Console.WriteLine("{0} / {1} = {2}", firstNum, sec
ondNum, result);

            Console.Write("Do you want to do more calc
ulations?(Yes/No): ");

            restart = Console.ReadLine();

            break;
```

```csharp
            case '%':

                result = firstNum % secondNum;

                Console.WriteLine("{0} % {1} = {2}", firstNum, se
condNum, result);

                Console.Write("Do you want to do more calc
ulations?(Yes/No): ");

                restart = Console.ReadLine();

                break;


        default:

                Console.Write("Invalid Operator! Do you want
to try again?(Yes/No): ");

                restart = Console.ReadLine();

                break;

        }

    }

    while(restart == "Yes" || restart == "yes");
```

```
        }

    }

}
```

Output:

Now we won't have to stop and re-run the program again in order to do more calculations.

```
Enter first number: 6
Enter second number: 9
Enter operator ( +, -, *, /, %): -
6 - 9 = -3
Do you want to do more calculations?(Yes/No): yes
Enter first number: 5
Enter second number: 4
Enter operator ( +, -, *, /, %): ?
Invalid Operator! Do you want to try again?(Yes/No): yes
Enter first number: 5
Enter second number: 4
Enter operator ( +, -, *, /, %): +
5 + 4 = 9
Do you want to do more calculations?(Yes/No): no
```

4.3: Summary

After completing chapter 4, we now have completed the flow control section, which includes loops. After that, we added a new feature to our calculator from section 3.4 by giving the user the option to do more calculations without stopping the program.

Chapter 5: Mistakes to avoid in Programming

In the last chapter, we will talk about common beginner programming mistakes and how to avoid them, and we are going to then continue our progress in C# by working with Arrays.

Before we get into the practice of writing clean and better code, let's take a look at some of its attributes.

1. A well-written program should be readable. If anyone else is reading your code, they can experience the same sensation as if they were reading a novel or poetry.

2. Code should be elegant and simple to read. It should be enjoyable to read and make you happy.

3. Clean code should be straightforward and quick to comprehend

Things to practice while coding:

1. **Use Meaningful naming conventions:** You probably noticed by now that while coding, you'll be naming many variables. Make a pattern of using meaningful words in your code. Only follow one naming case. For example, throughout this book, we utilized the camel case convention for variables.

2. **Avoid Writing Unnecessary Comments:** comments are beneficial to explain what part of a code to does. Code is

moved around during production. If the comment stays in the exact location, it can cause a significant issue. It may confuse the developers, and they may become distracted as a result of the irrelevant comments. It's not as if you shouldn't use comments at all. They're often necessary.

3. **Indentation:** In computer programming, indentation is used to format the statements inside a program for better readability. This can be helpful to visualize the follow of statements. Indentation is habitually only beneficial to programmers. Compilers and interpreters are usually unconcerned with the amount of whitespace between programming statements.

5.1 Arrays

An array is a set of variables of the same data type that share the same name. And each data piece is known as an array element. The data type of the array elements could be any of the data types we learned about, such as **char**, **int**, or **float**, and they are all stored in a single contiguous location. The array's length determines the array's element count.

In C#, memory is allocated dynamically for arrays. And since arrays are objects, it is simple to determine their length using pre-defined functions. The array's variables are arranged, and each array's index starts at 0. In C#, arrays behave in a unique way than they do in C++.

Things to remember about Arrays:

- All arrays are assigned dynamically in C#.

- Because arrays in C# are objects, we can determine their size using the member length property. This is in contrast to C++, where the size or length is determined using the **sizeof** function.

- Array variables in C# can also be declared similarly to other variables by placing **[]** after the data type.

- The array's elements are ordered, and each has an index starting at 0.

- The default values for numeric array and reference type items are zero and null, respectively.

- In C#, arrays are objects of the base type, **System.Array** Set of.

- Elements in an array can be of any data type (but all of them must be of the same kind), including an array type.

Array declaration/Syntax:

The general syntax of an array is:

```
< Data Type > [ ] < Name_Array >
```

Now for example we have an **array** of type **int** called *usersAge:*

```
//index:   0  1  2  3

int[] usersAge = {19, 26, 58, 22};
```

Do remember that declaration of an array doesn't allocate it memory, so it must have some initialized data in it

5.2: Accessing Elements of Array: manually

We may assign the value during initialization. However, after declaring and initializing the array, we can assign its value randomly using its index. We can access the value of an array by indexing; place the element's index within square brackets alongside the array name. suppose that we wanted to access the second element in usersAge array then we can do:

```
//declares and initializes int type array with a size of four (0 to 3)

    int[] usersAge = new int[3]

    // assign the value 19 in array on index 0

    usersAge[0] = 19;

    // assign the value 26 in array on index 1

    usersAge[1] = 26;
```

```
    // assign the value 58 in array on index 2

    usersAge[2] = 58;


    //returning values:

    usersAge[2];          // returns 58
```

The keyword **new** is used to assign memory. It isn't essential to use the new keyword to declare and initialize concurrently. However, the new keyword is essential after the declaration.

5.3: Accessing Elements of Array: using loops.

In the previous section, we learned to assign and print those values by writing every single element's index in an array, which is fine, but this is time costly, and to save time, we use loops which were covered in detail in the preceding chapter.

The code below prints all elements of an array using different types of loops:

```
using System;


namespace Arrays

{
```

```csharp
class myProgram

{

    public static void Main(string[] args)

    {

        // declaring an array of integers.

        int[] myArray;


        // allocating memory for 5 integers.

        myArray = new int[5];


        // initializing the elements of the array

        myArray[0] = 10;

        myArray[1] = 20;

        myArray[2] = 30;

        myArray[3] = 40;

        myArray[4] = 50;


        // using the for loop

        Console.Write("For loop :");
```

```csharp
for (int j = 0; j < myArray.Length; j++)

{

    Console.Write(" " + myArray[j]);

}

Console.WriteLine("");

Console.Write("For-each loop :");


// using the for-each loop

foreach(int i in myArray)

{

    Console.Write(" " + i);

}


Console.WriteLine("");

Console.Write("while loop :");


// using the while loop

int j = 0;

while (j < myArray.Length)
```

```csharp
        {
            Console.Write(" " + myArray[j]);

            j++;

        }


        Console.WriteLine("");
        Console.Write("Do-while loop :");


        // using the do-while loop
        int k = 0;
        do
        {

            Console.Write(" " + myArray[k]);

            k++;

        }

        while (k < myArray.Length);

    }

  }

}
```

Output:

```
For loop : 10 20 30 40 50
For-each loop : 10 20 30 40 50
while loop : 10 20 30 40 50
Do-while loop : 10 20 30 40 50
```

Saving user input in an array:

```csharp
using System;

namespace Arrays
{
    class myProgram
    {
        public static void Main(string[] args)
        {
            // declares an Array of integers.
            int[] myArray;

            // allocating memory for 3 integers.
            myArray = new int[3];       // total Length is 4
```

```csharp
// using the for loop

for (int x = 0; x < myArray.Length; x++)

{

    Console.Write("Enter element # " + x + ": ");

    myArray[x] = Convert.ToInt32(Console.ReadLine());


}

Console.Write("\vFor loop :");

for (int x = 0; x < myArray.Length; x++)

{

    Console.Write(" " + myArray[x]);

}



    }

  }

}
```

We can also perform the same task with other loops, but for loop or foreach loop is recommended when working with arrays in C#.

In the above code example, we used two for loops, one for entering data and the other for printing the output is as follows:

Output:

```
Enter element # 0: 5
Enter element # 1: 9
Enter element # 2: 4

For loop : 5 9 4
```

5.4: Types of Arrays

In C#, there are three main types of arrays:

- 1-D (one dimensional) arrays

- Multi-dimensional arrays

- Jagged arrays

One dimensional array:

The arrays we made in previous sections were all examples of one-dimensional or, in short, 1-D array. Now we already know how to declare a 1-D array, for example:

```
myArray = new int[3];
```

myArray is a 1-D array with index's 0 to 3. The new keyboard is responsible for creating the array and initializing its elements to their default values. In the preceding example, all elements are initialized to zero, as the int form is used. Given below is an example of a 1-D array

```
using System;

namespace Arrays
{
    class myProgram
    {
        public static void Main(string[] args)
        {
            // declaring a 1D Array of string.
            string[] myDays;

            // allocating memory for days.
            myDays = new string[] {"Monday", "Tuesday", "Wednesday", "Thursday", "Friday", "Saturday", "Sunday"};

            // Displaying Elements of array
            foreach(string day in weekDays)
```

```
        {
            Console.Write(day + " ");

        }


        }

    }
}
```

Output:

```
Monday Tuesday Wednesday Thursday Friday Saturday Sunday
```

Multi-dimensional arrays:

The multi-dimensional array includes several rows in which the values are stored. It is often referred to as a Rectangular Array in C# because each row has the same length. It may be a two-dimensional array, a three-dimensional array, or a multi-dimensional array. Nested loops are necessary to store and access the array's values. The declaration, initialization, and accessing of a multi-dimensional array are as follows:

```
// creates a 2-d array of three rows and five columns:

    int[, ] intarray = new int[3, 5];
```

```
//creates an array of 3-d, 5, 2, and 8:

    int[ , , ] intarray1 = new int[5, 2, 8];
```

The "," in the declaration of 2-D array shows that there are two lengths, one for row and other for columns and similar for the **3-D** array just that there is an extra argument and "," symbol, an easier way to remember this could be that and **3-D** array is just like a 3D object which three axes (x, y, z) and 2D array consists of two axes (x, y).

```
using System;


namespace Arrays

{

    class myProgram

    {

        public static void Main(string[] args)

        {


            // two dimensional:

            int[ , ] twoDArray = new int[3, 3];
```

```
twoDArray[0,1] = 20;

twoDArray[1,2] = 30;

twoDArray[2,0] = 40;


// three dimensional:

int [ , , ] threeDArray = new int[2, 2, 3] { { { 1, 2, 3 }, { 4, 5,
6 } }, { { 7, 8, 9 }, { 10, 11, 12 } } };


Console.WriteLine("\t\v2-D Arrray:");

for(int i = 0; i < 3; i++)

{

    for(int j = 0; j < 3; j++)

    {

        Console.Write( twoDArray[i, j] + " " );

    }

    Console.WriteLine();

}


    Console.WriteLine("\t\v3-D Arrray:");
```

```csharp
            Console.WriteLine("3DArray[0][0][0] : " + threeDArray[
0, 0, 0]);

            Console.WriteLine("3DArray[1][1][2] : " + threeDArray[
1, 1, 2]);

            Console.WriteLine("3DArray[0][1][1] : " + threeDArray[
0, 1, 1]);

            Console.WriteLine("3DArray[1][0][2] : " + threeDArray[
1, 0, 2]);

    }

}
}
```

Output:

```
            2-D Arrray:
0 20 0
0 0 30
40 0 0


            3-D Arrray:
3DArray[0][0][0] : 1
3DArray[1][1][2] : 12
3DArray[0][1][1] : 5
3DArray[1][0][2] : 9
```

Jagged arrays

A jagged array consists of elements that are also arrays; *the term "array of arrays" refers to such an array*. Elements of the jagged array can have varying dimensions and sizes. The examples below demonstrate how to declare, initialize, and access elements of jagged arrays.

```
using System;

namespace Arrays
{
    class myProgram
    {
        public static void Main(string[] args)
        {

            // Declaring the array of two elements:
            int[][] firstArray = new int[2][];

            // Initializing the elements:
```

```csharp
        firstArray[0] = new int[5] { 1, 3, 5, 7, 9 };

        firstArray[1] = new int[4] { 2, 4, 6, 8 };


        // Another way of Declaring and initialing of elements

        int[][] secondArray = { new int[] { 1, 3, 5, 7, 9 }, new int[] { 2, 4, 6, 8 } };


        // Display the array elements:
        for (int k = 0; i < firstArray.Length; k++)
        {
            Console.Write("Element #" + i + " Array: ");
            for (int j = 0; j < firstArray[k].Length; j++)
            {
                Console.Write(firstArray[k][j] + " ");
            }
            Console.WriteLine();
        }
```

```csharp
        Console.WriteLine("\vAnother Array");


        // Display the the new array's elements:

        for (int i = 0; i < secondArray.Length; i++)

        {

            Console.Write("Element #" + i + " Array: ");

            for (int j = 0; j < secondArray[i].Length; j++)

            {

                Console.Write(secondArray[i][j] + " ");

            }

            Console.WriteLine();

        }

    }

}
}
```

Output:

```
Element #0 Array: 1 3 5 7 9
Element #1 Array: 2 4 6 8

Another Array
Element #0 Array: 1 3 5 7 9
Element #1 Array: 2 4 6 8
```

5.5: Summary

In the last chapter of this book, we learned the core concept of arrays, accessing elements and printing elements, saving user's input in an array, three types of arrays: *1-D, multi-dimensional,* and *jagged arrays*.

Conclusion

First of all, congratulations on completing this book. Now that you have learned almost all of the programming fundamentals, you can move into advanced topics like Structs and OOP (classes and objects) or look into more specific issues of your interests.